IMAGES
of America

POMPANO
BEACH

Veteran harness driver George Sholty has just won the sixth race with Buster Tass at Pompano Park, December 17, 1971. He looks to his left at the score board to check his winning time. Pompano Park has often been designated as the world capital of harness racing.

IMAGES
of America

POMPANO
BEACH

Frank J. Cavaioli

ARCADIA
PUBLISHING

Published by Arcadia Publishing
Charleston, South Carolina

Library of Congress Catalog Card Number: 2001091341

For all general information contact Arcadia Publishing at:
Telephone 843-853-2070
Fax 843-853-0044
E-mail sales@arcadiapublishing.com
For customer service and orders:
Toll-Free 1-888-313-2665

Visit us on the Internet at www.arcadiapublishing.com

A palm tree, a fish, and the sea adorn a distinctive Pompano Beach logo atop City Hall at Atlantic Boulevard.

CONTENTS

INTRODUCTION

Pompano Beach, located in Broward County, has grown from swampland to modern urban center in the southeastern region of Florida. This region combines the counties of Palm Beach, Broward, and Miami-Dade. Pompano was incorporated in 1908. In 1947 the towns of Pompano and Pompano Beach were merged into the City of Pompano Beach.

The first inhabitants of Pompano Beach were Native Americans, thought to be Tequestas. The old Indian Mound at the northeast border of Lake Santa Barbara has been recognized as a site where Indians lived. The completion of the Pompano Canal (a part of the Intracoastal Waterway) in 1890 from Jupiter to Biscayne Bay and the coming of the Flagler Florida East Coast Railway in 1896 contributed to the community's development.

Early pioneers settled around Lettuce Lake, now known as Lake Santa Barbara. Frank Sheene named the city "Pompano" after the plentiful fish found in the area. Pompano was originally part of Dade County until 1909, then Palm Beach County until 1915, and then part of Broward County when the latter was formed in 1915.

William L. Kester (1873–1954) greatly influenced Pompano's development. Upon retiring from the north he moved to Miami, then to Fort Lauderdale, and eventually settled in Pompano in 1923 to enjoy the area's fishing and golf. Not content to remain idle, he invested in various enterprises. The hurricanes of 1926 and 1928 set him back temporarily. He was elected to a two-year term on the city council, engaged in farming and cattle raising, and established a construction company. He boosted tourism when he built more than 100 vacation cottages. Most of the Kester Cottages have been torn down, but several remain scattered around the city.

Pompano experienced a building boom in the 1920s, but economic decline began in late 1925. The first Pompano Track was built in 1926; it was immediately shut down because pari-mutuel betting was illegal until 1931. It was on February 4, 1964, that the modern Pompano Park opened on a permanent basis to become the "Capital of Harness Racing." It continues today with year-round live racing, simulcasting, and dining, while it hosts other events such as the Broward County Fair and the National Antique Car Show.

The 1930 census reported 2,614 Pompano inhabitants. The Walton Hotel, which opened in 1926 during the Florida boom, was the earliest free-standing hotel, three stories high, and located near the Florida East Coast Railway and Farmers Market. Business leaders roomed there, politicians stopped to give speeches, and it was the center of social activity. The Walton Hotel was purchased by the First Baptist Church and was torn down in the 1980s.

In 1940 the population reached 4,427. The year before, the Pompano State Farmers Market was opened and placed under control of the Florida Department of Agriculture. It expanded rapidly and is now located on a 21-acre site with a new three-story administration building at Interstate 95 and Atlantic Boulevard.

The 1950 population reached 5,682. Storyland Amusement Park was opened in 1955 at South Federal Highway, across from Lake Santa Barbara. This attraction preceded Disney World by more than a decade. Storyland Park was closed and razed in 1964. The Pompano Beach Chamber of Commerce was established in 1947. In 1960 there were 15,992 people living in the city.

The Pompano Beach Air Park, owned by the City of Pompano Beach, provides general aviation services. Begun in 1938, the park served the Naval Air Station at Fort Lauderdale. After World War II the city acquired the airport. The Goodyear Blimp leases 32.5 acres west of the Air Park and is a familiar sight to residents and millions of television viewers during special events. The census reported the population at 39,012 in 1970 and 52,618 in 1980.

At a 1940 Rotary meeting, retired librarian and teacher Effie Power urged the participants to start a library. A committee was formed to implement this charge and included Rev. George Foster, Mrs. T.N. Alexander, Mrs. William H. Blount, Van E. Malcolm, E. Guy Owens, and Effie Power. In April the Pompano Public Library opened in temporary facilities. In 1956 the present site at Thirteenth Street was opened.

Pompano Beach has had a rich multicultural history. Blanche Ely founded the first school for African Americans on Hammondville Road, and the Blanche Ely High School honors her memory. E. Pat Larkins graduated from this school in 1960 and later served as commissioner and mayor of the City of Pompano Beach for 20 years. Pompano Beach's first black museum was established in 2000 in the Ely home. The Ely Educational Museum is located in the three-bedroom home of Blanche Ely at Northwest Fifteenth Street and Northwest Sixth Avenue. Joseph Ely was the first principal of Fort Lauderdale's Old Dillard High School. In 1942 Professor Ely, working with the help of his wife, Blanche, and Clarence Walker, helped to get Broward County to extend the school year from September to June. Previously, black schools were closed for part of the school year because of the need for agricultural labor.

The Reverend James E. Coleman (1873–1958) of the Mt. Calvary Baptist Church was honored for his dedicated community work when Coleman Park was named after him at the site where Coleman Elementary School had been. Award-winning actress Esther Rolle was born in a "section house" and grew up in Pompano in a family of farmers. In 1981, Northwest Third Avenue was named Esther Rolle Avenue in her honor.

After 1960 population growth shifted eastward as oceanfront condominiums were built. For example, the Renaissance I and II condominiums, each 28 stories high, were completed in 1974 and 1976, respectively. The number of retail stores expanded and shoppers patronized Beachway, Oceanside, Beacon Light, and Pompano Fashion Square. The businesses in the old commercial district along Flagler and First Street declined. Agriculture also suffered after World War II.

The construction of two retirement villages added to the expansion and attraction of Pompano Beach. The John Knox Village opened in the 1970s and consists of garden apartments, apartments, and villas on 54 acres. Upon putting down a sum of money to the Village Endowment, adults were guaranteed home maintenance, recreation, and nursing care. The other large active adult community is Palm Aire. Begun in the 1950s it expanded its facilities to include a population of 6,000 and boasted a spa, hotel, golf courses, restaurants, pro shops, and a country club.

One of the most successful continuous traditions is the Pompano Beach Fishing Rodeo, which celebrated its 36th year in 2001. Conducted each May, it has since become the largest saltwater tournament in South Florida and has donated its profits to marine conservation. The Annual Holiday Boat Show is another ongoing popular tradition. It has been held each December since 1962.

Pompano Beach is also known for its distinctive historic homes. The typical method of home construction was the frame vernacular style and was used in over 70 percent of the locally built environment. Considered ordinary architecture, it uses the builder's knowledge of the community and available materials. Examples of vernacular buildings are the Ben Turner House and the Captain Campbell House. The Bahamian frame vernacular architecture, evident in the city's Northwest section, is characterized by hip roofs, double hung sash windows, and front porches.

The Horace Robinson House in Old Pompano was constructed with Dade County pine in 1924 and is credited with being the birthplace of the South Florida Symphony. Examples of prairie vernacular architecture are the Harry McNab House and the Robert McNab House, which were built in 1926; they remain intact with a yellow brick façade and are characterized by horizontal lines, hipped roofs with wide overhangs, squared porch columns, and broad flat chimneys.

Albert Neale Sample built a two-story house on North Dixie Highway in 1916. Sample Road was laid out for his extensive farming operation, which stretched to the western edge of Broward County. William D. and Sarah McDougald purchased the house in 1943. The McDougald family donated the house to the Sample-McDougald Preservation Society, which had the house moved to 450 Northeast Tenth Street to serve as a living museum.

ACKNOWLEDGMENTS

I would like to thank the following people for their assistance in the production of this book: Patti Carr, Bud Garner, Kathleen G. Kelleher, Stewart R. Kester, Kay McGinn, Lillian Movsessian, Janice Rolle, and Carol H. Scott.

One

BEGINNINGS

This panoramic view of the Kester Ocean Colony on North Ocean Boulevard was taken in 1950. The 45 two- and three-bedroom furnished cottages promoted tourism for Pompano Beach. Notice that there is no development along the beach at this time.

COME TO POMPANO

Free Auto Trip!   Free Presents!

The Season's Opportunity in Land Values!

Autos Will Leave
HOTEL GILBERT 11:30 A. M.
Friday, January 22.   The Trip is Free!

Dinner will be Served by the Ladies of the Pompano Civic Association

Free Pianos; Guaranteed Ladies' and Gentlemen's Gold Watches and Other Presents will be Distributed Absolutely FREE!

But the Biggest Inducement is your opportunity to buy at Your Own Price a piece of valuable Florida Real Estate. Business Lots in the Thriving Town of Pompano, and Farm Property nearby, at Your Own Valuation.

Do Not Forget
CASSEL'S HAMMOCK

the Finest Citrus Fruit and Vegetable Land to be found in Palm Beach county. Land no better sells at one to two thousand dollars per acre. You make the price on this. Everything must go at bidder's figure.

Sale will be conducted by
DAMMERS & GILLETTE
Famous New York Auctioneers.

Remember the Date: JANUARY 22 and 23.
If the weather should be bad, the Sale will be held the first good day.

A very prominent advertisement of January 22 and 23, 1915, announces the advantages of moving to Pompano. It represented the first attempt to start a land boom in the community's history. It was also a time when Pompano lacked the amenities of a modern municipality.

The Intracoastal Waterway, before it became a marine avenue, can be seen extending north to south with the Atlantic Ocean to the left in the background. This rare scene shows Pompano Beach in a pristine setting before the early settlers established community life. Today nearly all the oceanfront land and the Intracoastal Waterway have been developed for the benefit of visitors and residents alike.

While Pompano was beginning its development, areas to the south were advancing more rapidly. Here the Tallyho Bus prepares to go on a sightseeing tour from the Hollywood Country Club in 1924.

11

The Tequesta Indians occupied the area from Pompano to Cape Sable. The Indian Mound located at Southeast Thirteenth Street and Hibiscus Avenue is believed to be 2,000 years old. Skeletal remains and an old wooden image known as the "Keeper of the Mound" were found at this site in Indian Mound Park in 1938 by archaeologist John Goggin.

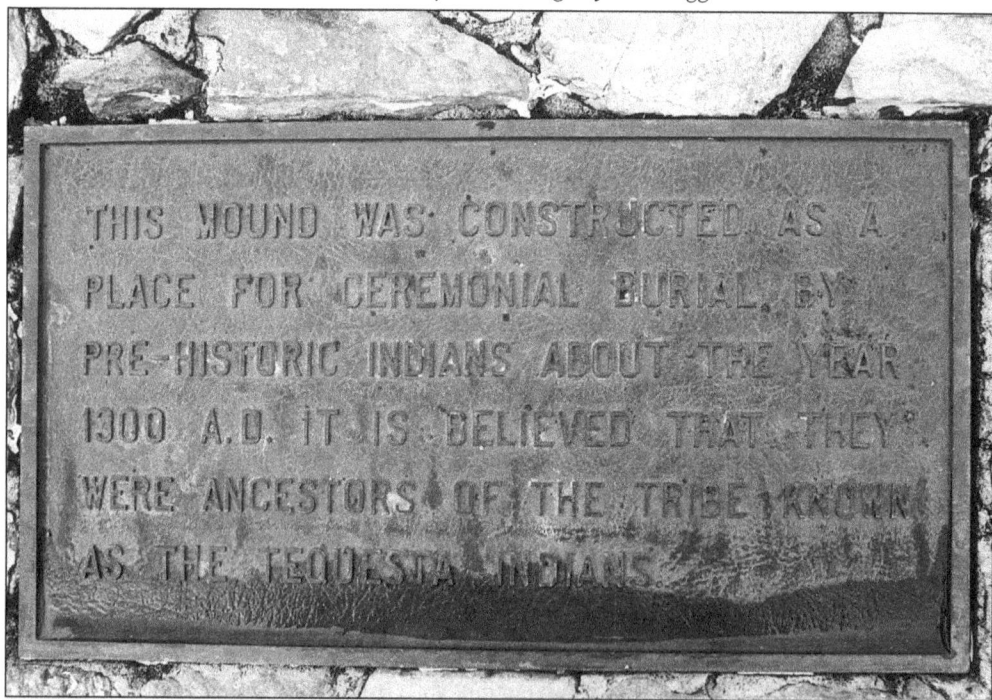

THIS MOUND WAS CONSTRUCTED AS A PLACE FOR CEREMONIAL BURIAL BY PRE-HISTORIC INDIANS ABOUT THE YEAR 1300 A.D. IT IS BELIEVED THAT THEY WERE ANCESTORS OF THE TRIBE KNOWN AS THE TEQUESTA INDIANS

A historical marker, located at the top of the Indian Mound, proclaims that a Native American ceremonial site was built here. Today Indian Mound Park is a passive park in Pompano Beach.

Devastation is clearly evident after the hurricane of September 18, 1926 at the Ogden Building at First Street and Flagler Avenue. Another storm struck Pompano two years later.

W.H. McNab Sr., left, and R.A. McNab, right, relax in front of their gas station on Atlantic Boulevard and Federal Highway. They settled in Pompano in 1898 to farm and lived in a palmetto shack on the beach before they built their yellow brick houses on opposite sides of Atlantic Boulevard.

J.E. Garner moved to Pompano in 1926 and became a section (track) foreman with the Florida East Coast Railroad. He is the father of Bud Garner, a Pompano Beach folklorist. The section foreman supervised five workers on a six-mile section of track.

This is a representation of the Florida East Coast Railroad section foreman's house near Flagler Street. It existed from 1896 until 1969, when it was torn down. The house lacked running water until 1947.

This statue of the "Barefoot Mailman" is situated at the administration building of the Town of Hillsboro Beach, north of Pompano Beach on State Road A1A. A mailman by the name of James Hamilton delivered mail by boat and by walking barefoot on the beach. He either drowned or was killed by an alligator in 1887 while attempting to swim across Hillsboro Inlet to reach Pompano because his skiff had disappeared. In 1956 the Hamilton post office substation at Riverside Drive was named in his honor.

The Hillsboro Lighthouse was erected in 1907 and stands majestically at the Hillsboro Inlet, the body of water connecting the Intracoastal Waterway to the Atlantic Ocean at the northern point of Pompano Beach. The lighthouse continues to operate as an indispensable navigational aid for mariners and ships along the east coast of Florida.

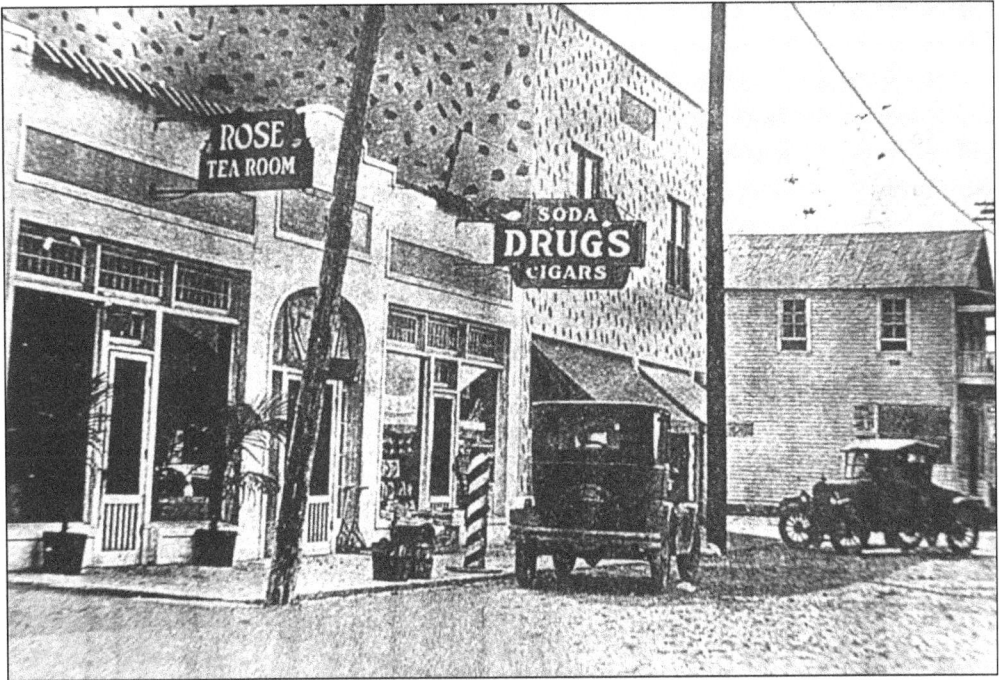

The center of Old Pompano business activity in the 1920s was at Northeast Flagler Avenue and First Street, east of the railroad. Note the dirt road upon which these vintage automobiles had to maneuver.

The administration building and parking area of the original Pompano Race Track are shown here on November 11, 1926. The State forced it to close because pari-mutuel betting was illegal until 1931.

The Pompano Beach Historical Monument stands in front of the civic center on Sixth Street. It was dedicated on May 29, 1999, to the men and women who settled in the city between 1896 and 1921. The sign to the right announces events for the amphitheater located behind the civic center.

18

This monument is dedicated to the memory of those men and women, known and unknown, who came to this area between 1896 and 1921. These pioneers came to farm or engage in commerce in the Pompano settlement. They chose to make their home in this warm place of rich soil, abundant fish, pines, palmettos, alligators and mosquitos. They were in many ways a diverse group, but all had the determination to endure the harsh conditions. Each pioneer family was very important in our history and contributed to the development of Pompano Beach.

It is said that a railroad surveyor gave the name "Pompano" to the area in honor of the delicious fish he had eaten here. The Town of Pompano was incorporated in 1908, and became the City of Pompano Beach in 1947.

Pompano Beach Historical Society   May 29, 1999

Co-Chairmen Donald Downie and Eldes Walton Whitsett.
Mercelene A. Rutledge - Cornelius Rolle

Funded by Descendants and Pompano High School Alumni, the "Beanpickers"

William L. Kester is also recognized for his many contributions to our city.

This plaque stands at the base of the Pompano Beach Historical Monument on Sixth Street and honors the pioneer families that settled in this area of South Florida. Frank Sheene, an early settler and railroad surveyor, gave the town its name, "Pompano," after he had eaten the delicious local fish.

Alexander, F. L.	Hammon, H. F.
Alexander, Tonnie	Hardin, D. J.
Armbrister, David	Hardin, R. A.
Ashley, G. W.	Hardy, I. I.
Austin, F. S.	Harper, L. G.
Bailey, B. F.	Harry, A. E.
Baker, Tom	Harry, Jesse
Beville, T. Sol	Helton, R. C.
Bland, Clyde	Helton, R. F.
Blount, J. D.	Henderson, H. H.
Blount, G. L.	Heynes, W. A.
Blount, W. H.	Higgs, Maynard
Butler, G. O.	Hinson, C. D. "Col.
Campbell, H. "Cap"	Hogan, A. S.
Carson, F. M.	Holland, Walter
Cassells, W. B.	Howell, J. K.
Chapman, T. H.	Humphrey, R. L.
Cheshire, C. B.	Humphrey, S. B.
Cheshire, M. A.	Isler, J. B.
Cheshire, W. B.	Jelks, G. J.
Cole, N. D.	Johns, J. B.
Courson, J. E.	Johnson, O. K.
Courson, J. M.	Keene, J. R.
Curry, W. B.	Kneeland, Harry
Dorman, J. A.	Knight, E. T. "Cap"
Ely, Rev. Lawrence	Knight, Thomas
Folsom, Calib	Kunze, A. A.
French, J. D.	Lampp, E. R.
Gates, Willie	Lyons, C. L.
Hamilton, J. T.	Marshall, Carlton
Hamilton, S. M.	Mobley, E. A.

McClellan, Dr. George	Sheene, F. S.
McComb, James	Shiver, A. J.
McCullough, J. A.	Shiver, J. T.
McNab, R. A.	Shiver, N. T.
McNab, W. H.	Shuford, W. H.
Miller, G. H.	Simmons, G. F.
Mickler, C. A.	Simmons, J. E.
Mizel, J. R.	Skeen, S. B.
Osteen, A. A.	Slaughter, S. H.
Payton, Harry	Smith, Dexter,
Parnell, Roy	Smith, Dave
Peacock, J. K.	Smith, T. W.
Petsch, W. A.	Smith, W. E.
Pierce, J. W.	Smoak, J. P.
Pierce, P. M.	Snell, G. B.
Raines, T. E.	Speir, L. D.
Raines, W. H.	Sutton, H. M.
Rhone, John	Swain, Jack
Richardson, A. L.	Thurston, Joe
Richardson, William	Tillis, J. H.
Riggs, J. H.	Tinney, Oliver
Robinson, Horace	Turner, A. W.
Robinson, Wallace	Umstead, J. W.
Rogers, E.	Walton, G. R.
Rolle, E. R.	Walton, J. W.
Rolle, J. R.	Waldron, R. L.
Rouse, G. W.	Warren, J. L.
Russell, Elijah	Warren, L. S.
Sample, A. N.	Williams, W. T.
Saxon, J. A.	Wyse, G. D.
Saxon, O. W.	

This list of names honors the first settlers who arrived between 1896 to 1921. Their names are permanently inscribed at the historical monument at the civic center. Many of their descendants still live in Pompano Beach. The work of the Pompano Beach Historical Society and the Pioneer Days event help to preserve the heritage of the past.

THE BELL FAMILY	THE HORN FAMILY
THE BLUE FAMILY	THE McDOUGLE FAMILY
THE CARTER FAMILY	THE MILLER FAMILY
THE CASON FAMILY	THE MOORE FAMILY
THE CLARK FAMILY	THE NELSON FAMILY
THE CROCKETT FAMILY	THE NEWBOLD FAMILY
THE DURHAM FAMILY	THE PAYTON FAMILY
THE EDMOND FAMILY	THE RAWLS FAMILY
THE ELLINGTON FAMILY	THE ROLLE FAMILY
THE GARNETT FAMILY	THE RUSSELL FAMILY
THE GARY FAMILY	THE SCRUGGS FAMILY
THE GATES FAMILY	THE SWAIN FAMILY
THE GILLIS FAMILY	THE THOMPSON FAMILY
THE GOODWIN FAMILY	THE WAY FAMILY
THE GOSS FAMILY	THE WELLS FAMILY
THE GRAHAM FAMILY	THE WOOTEN FAMILY
THE HIGGS FAMILY	

The names on this plaque represent the pioneer families who lived in the Northwest section of Pompano Beach. Their contributions helped to establish a successful community, and the names are familiar to many residents who recall memorable events of the past.

Constructed in 1926, this building served as the Pompano Central School, the high school, and the junior high school over the years until 1972, when it was torn down. The building was located between Third and Fourth Avenues and Fourth and Sixth Streets.

Bud Garner is proud to be a leader among the active pioneer families. Here he stands in front of the Kester Cottages in Founders Park. Considered a folklorist, Garner is famous for his chronicles of Old Pompano.

Pioneer Harley "Cap" Campbell was an early Pompano settler. To the right he is seen as a young man, and to the left just before his death. Campbell was a successful farmer, realtor, and politician. His house was built in 1910 and remains one of the oldest structures in Pompano Beach.

An original wall phone has been preserved in one of the historic Kester Cottages, now a museum, at Founders Park. The two Kester Cottages at Founders Park were built, along with more than 100 others, in the 1930s for vacationers. They were moved from other parts of the city to preserve the heritage of an earlier era.

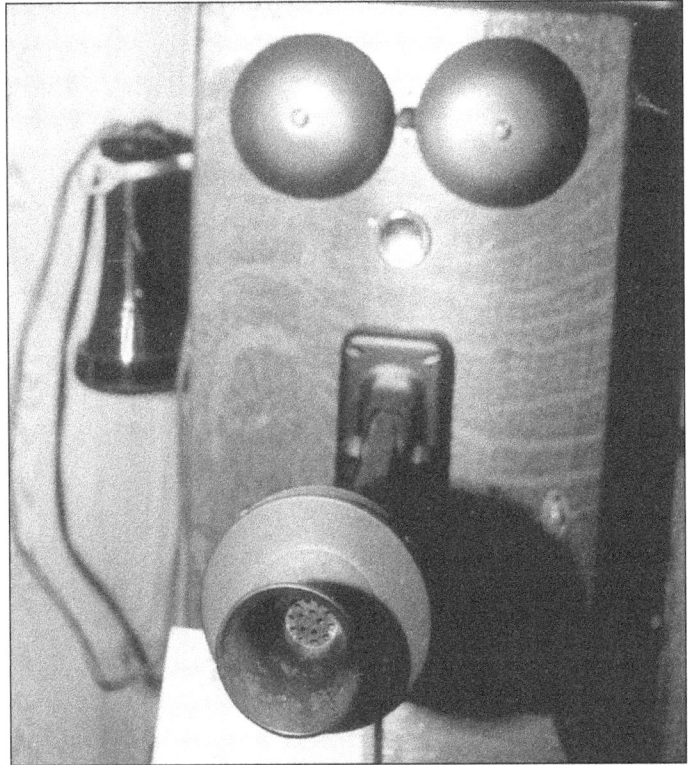

Eldes Walton Whitsett, left, and Kay McGinn, right, pause for a moment with a 1930s costumed mannequin in the Kester Cottage Museum at Founders Park. Whitsett is a descendant of the Walton pioneer family, and McGinn is a city commissioner.

Jack Faulkner, kneeling next to his dog Contact, prepares to take off to dust the fields in 1936. His assistant, Jim Crawford, stands to the left. Faulkner later died when his car crashed into Cypress Creek where he was trapped and drowned. This scene is the location of today's John Knox Village.

This is the complete directory of the Southern Bell Telephone Company for Pompano as it looked in 1927. The directory consisted of one page and has survived in this condition as a testimony of an earlier period. Several important earlier settlers such as the Blounts and Robinsons are listed here.

William L. Kester, shown in this rare photo, settled in Pompano in 1923 to enjoy fishing and retirement after a productive career with the Westinghouse corporation and in a brokerage house. However, not content to be retired, he became active in civic and business affairs and helped to shape early Pompano. The "Kester Cottages" he built promoted tourism on the beach. In 1974 William's nephew, Stewart R. Kester, donated two "Kester Cottages" to be the foundation of a historical museum at Founders Park.

This attractively landscaped house belonged to William L. Kester. It was located two blocks south of the present Fourteenth Street Bridge on the ocean side of Twelfth Avenue. Kester served on the city council, built the Kester Building on Old Dixie Highway, and donated land for the development of the library, garden club, Episcopal church, cemetery, municipal athletic field, and Pioneer Park.

William L. Kester's immediate family consisted of his mother, left; his brother Robert L. Kester, center; and his brother Clay Kester, right. They posed for this picture in the 1930s at William's home south of the Fourteenth Street Bridge at Twelfth Avenue. The Kester brothers were enthusiastic boosters of Pompano's development and expansion. The Pompano census of population in 1940 reached 4,427.

Two

A SETTLEMENT GROWS

The Pompano State Farmers Market opened in 1939 on Hammond Road. It soon became the largest winter produce market. Most of the business involved bell peppers, cucumbers, and squash. Today it is located on a 21-acre site at Interstate 95 and Atlantic Boulevard. This 1940s photo depicts the world's largest vegetable platform.

This is the first advisory committee from Tallahassee for the Pompano Beach State Farmers Market. They are, from left to right, Hiram Bakes, Walter Clark, C.B. Cheshire, J.A. Allison, G.B. Hogan, Nathan Mayo (agricultural commissioner), P.L. Hinson, Harvey Cheshire, unidentified, and Frank Delegel.

This is the Florida East Coast Railroad Station at the corner of North Dixie Highway and Hammondville Road (Third Street). It was a favorite destination for travelers to Old Pompano. The building was demolished in 1968.

The old Bank of Pompano stands at unpaved First Avenue and First Street. It was robbed of more than $10,000 on a hot September day in 1924 by the notorious Ashley Gang. John Ashley and his three associates were later gunned down at Sebastian, but the money was never recovered.

The Hillsboro Lighthouse just north of Pompano Beach stands guard at the inlet for the safe navigation of ships. This famous landmark has survived hurricanes and remains intact to this day. It was erected in 1907, and the first lighthouse keeper was Alfred A. Berghell.

The Pompano Beach Bathing Pavilion and Dance Casino at Briny Avenue and Atlantic Boulevard was built by the City in 1940 at a cost of $15,000. It provided facilities for dressing rooms, showers, dancing, and dining that overlooked the ocean. It also served as the first home of the Pompano Beach Elks Lodge 1898. At top is the dining room. The building was destroyed by fire November 27, 1954. Pompano's population in 1950 was 5,682.

This illustration depicts an active State Farmers Market in Pompano Beach during the early years of the 1940s. The enterprise in American agricultural productivity and distribution became an immediate success after the market's inception in 1939. Note the large number of bushels and the overflowing beans and peppers in those bushels.

The telephone switchboard operator is busy in the State Farmers Market office in 1940. The two young ladies facing each other take a break from their work.

The Pompano Beach Bean and Pepper Jamboree celebrated the end of the growing season each April at the State Farmers Market. This festive occasion featured games, exhibits, and plenty of delicious food. The event ended in 1953.

The Walton Hotel, built in 1925, was the center of business and social activity during Pompano's middle years. It was near the F.E.C. Railroad and the State Farmers Market at Northeast First Avenue and First Street. It was also the place for important political gatherings. The hotel was acquired by the First Baptist Church in 1980 and soon torn down to make way for a parking lot.

William L. Kester (1873–1954) settled in Pompano in 1923. He remained active in business and social affairs and became a city booster as he promoted tourism in the 1930s and 1940s. He built more than 100 cottages near the beach north of Atlantic Boulevard, many of which can be seen here in 1940. Hillsboro Lighthouse is barely visible in the distance at the top.

A cookout was conducted by the Lions Club at Kester Park in 1946. Leading participants and organizers of the cookout are, from left to right, Ord Green, Peter Austin, Bryan Rocker, Coye Cheshire, Angelo Thenos, Albert Smoak, E.E. Hardy, and Bobby McClellan.

These 1940 Lighthouse Cove apartments were located at the northeast section of Pompano. The Atlantic Ocean is in the background. It was a time when community leaders were striving to make Pompano a tourist destination.

Bud Garner (left), Thurman Bel (right), and Thurman's son Mark (center) display their catch of Lake Okeechobee bass in 1949. Fishing in South Florida was an important sport to residents and tourists alike.

This Sinclair gas station, a thriving business, was located at Northeast First Street and Northeast First Avenue in 1944. Notice the automobile raised on the old-fashioned lift in the background to the right. This gas station, typical of the World War II era, was primitive compared to today's modern facilities.

ROBERT L. McNAB
MEMORIAL PARK

THIS PROPERT
DONATED TO
THE CITY OF
POMPANO BEACH

IN LASTING MEMORY
OF THOSE WHO GAVE
THEIR LIVES
IN THE SERVICE
OF THEIR COUNTRY

W. H. McNAB AND R. A. McNAB

DEDICATED
THIS 22ND DAY OF FEBRUARY
1952 A.D.

This historical marker designates the Robert L. McNab Memorial Park at 2250 East Atlantic Boulevard to honor Pompano pioneers W.H. McNab and R.A. McNab. They came to Pompano from Winter Haven to farm, but they also engaged in real estate, contracting, and packing. In addition to the park, the family name has been preserved on a school and a road. The pair's yellow brick homes stand on the north and south side of Atlantic Boulevard at Northeast Eighteenth Street.

Bean pickers are working hard harvesting beans on this Pompano farm in 1944. The term "bean picker" at first meant migrant worker but later was adopted by the Pompano Beach High School athletic teams. The abundant agricultural produce contributed to the area's prosperity.

The 100 block of First Street in Old Pompano in the 1950s was part of the commercial center of the area. Soon after, business shifted eastward as a result of the construction of new shopping centers and high-rise condominiums closer to the beach.

Pompano's first fire truck, in the foreground, was built by the American La France Company of Elmira, New York, and Fire Chief F.A. Hunter took delivery July 1926, at a cost of $13,000. The truck had a pumping capacity of 750 gallons a minute, but it could only carry 100 gallons in its water tank. There were no fire hydrants then and bucket brigades helped to fight fires.

Pompano's first fire truck was in service from 1926 until 1948. It is shown here in a restored condition in the old fire house, which is now the Fire Museum at Founders Park. After many years of neglect and decay the fire truck was restored by a volunteer group of firefighters.

These smiling Pompano Beach school children posed for this group in 1950. The photo was accompanied by this statement: "Where the future citizens of Pompano are being molded."

Mrs. T.N. (Sue) Alexander served as a member of the Library Board for more than 40 years. As a community leader, she gave valuable service and guidance in garden clubs, the Methodist Church, and the Zonta Club.

These civic leaders attend a 1952 Pompano Beach Library meeting. They are, from left to right, Effie Powers, Dora McNab, Edna Welch, Josephine Peabody, and Mary Beal.

Ora L. Jones was a writer-journalist-printer who was also a local booster. He wrote *Some Glimpses of Pompano Beach*, a short history for the City's Golden Jubilee (1908–1958). He was originally from North Carolina. He died on July 10, 1971.

Long lines of boats move gingerly along the Intracoastal Waterway south of Atlantic Boulevard in 1952. The waterway serves as an avenue for pleasure boating and commercial traffic. The empty lot to the right in the foreground is the area where the Episcopal church is located. Note the relative lack of development at this time.

The Pompano Air Park is owned by the City and serves the area as a general aviation facility. It was deeded to Pompano Beach by the federal government at the close of World War II. The many parked planes at the Air Park reveal how busy this aviation center is. It has greatly expanded its service since this photo was taken in 1968. The air park lies east of Federal Highway and north of Tenth Avenue.

These smiling students are part of the 1938 eighth grade class of the Pompano Colored School. They are, from left to right, as follows: (front row) Verdell Thompson, Ruby Lewis, Cornelius Rolle, Katie Doby, and Annie Mae Cosslin; (back row) Thursta Mae Grooms, Susie Adams, Lucille Payne, Samuel Thomas, Ruby Edwards, and Mary Thornton.

42

Young Dennis McNab, grandson of Robert McNab, rides Old Gray, the family mule. This picture was taken on his grandfather's farm on South Federal Highway, east of the entrance to Imperial Point in 1938.

Bill Longino stands next to his crop duster plane "Prenar" in the 1930s. Since agriculture was then the most important business in Pompano, he and other pilots were kept busy dusting crops.

43

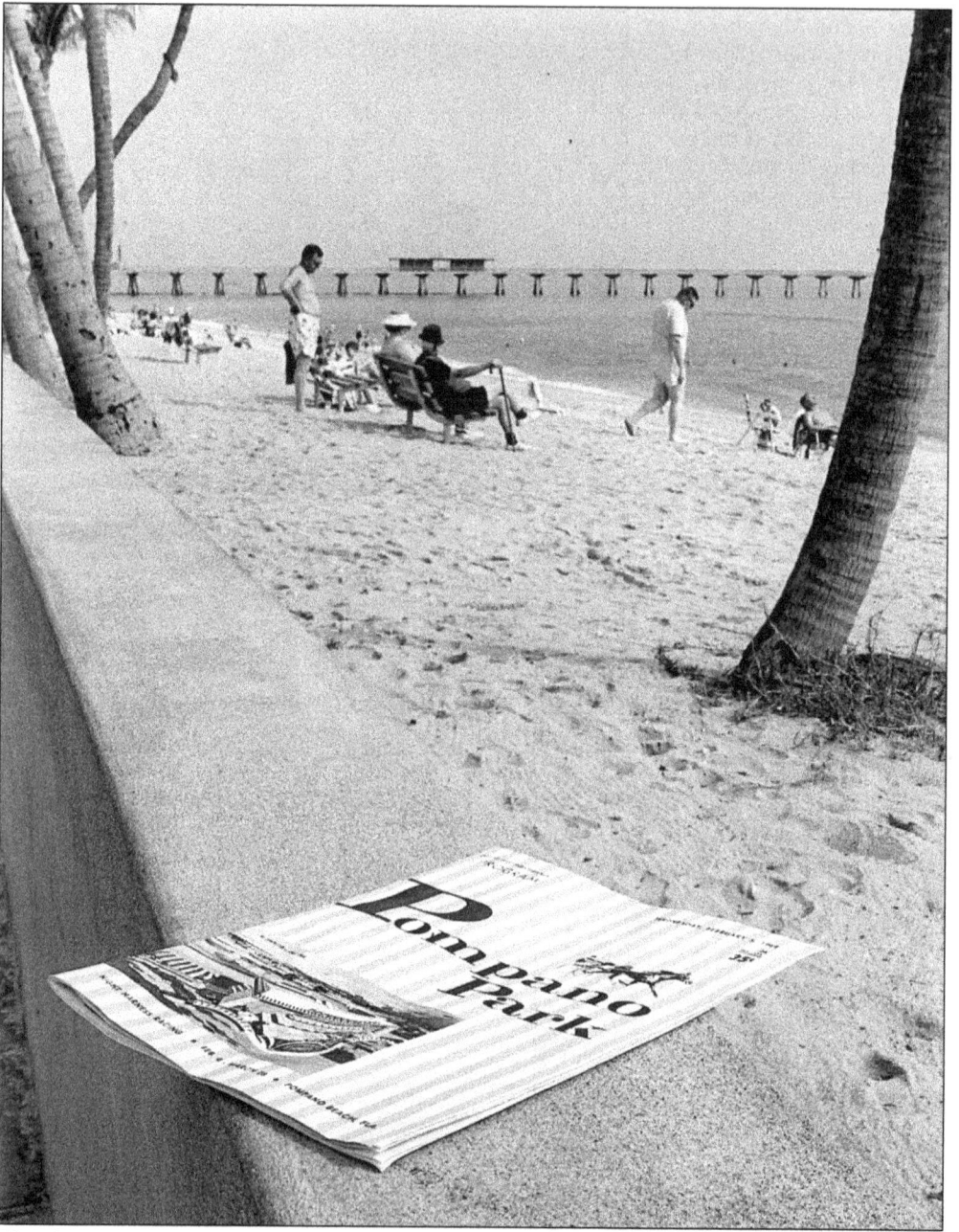

The first Pompano park program for the park's inaugural night of February 4, 1964, rests on a concrete wall at Pompano Beach. An unfinished pier is in the background, soon to be completed. Barely visible in the distance, to the left, is the Hillsboro Lighthouse. Pompano Park, the beach, and the lighthouse have all been an important part of the history of Pompano Beach.

Three

DEVELOPING A
COMMUNITY IDENTITY

The Pompano Beach High School Golden Tornadoes 1960–1961 basketball team pose for this photo. From 1928 to 1957 the athletic teams were known as the Beanpickers to signify the agricultural beginnings of the community. The students considered Beanpickers inappropriate and voted to replace it with the new designation of Tornadoes.

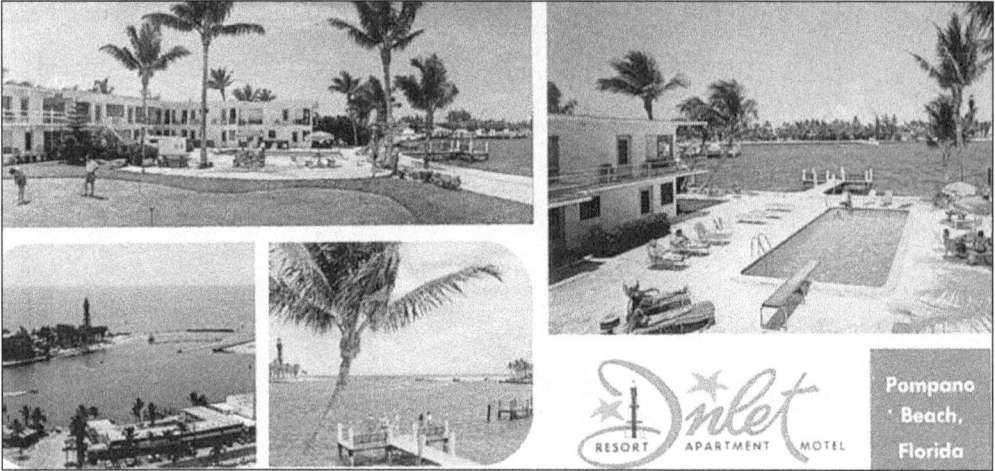

This composite view of northeast Pompano Beach at the Hillsboro Inlet captures the recreational attractions at the Inlet Resort Apartment Motel around 1970. The Hillsboro Lighthouse can be clearly seen in several panels.

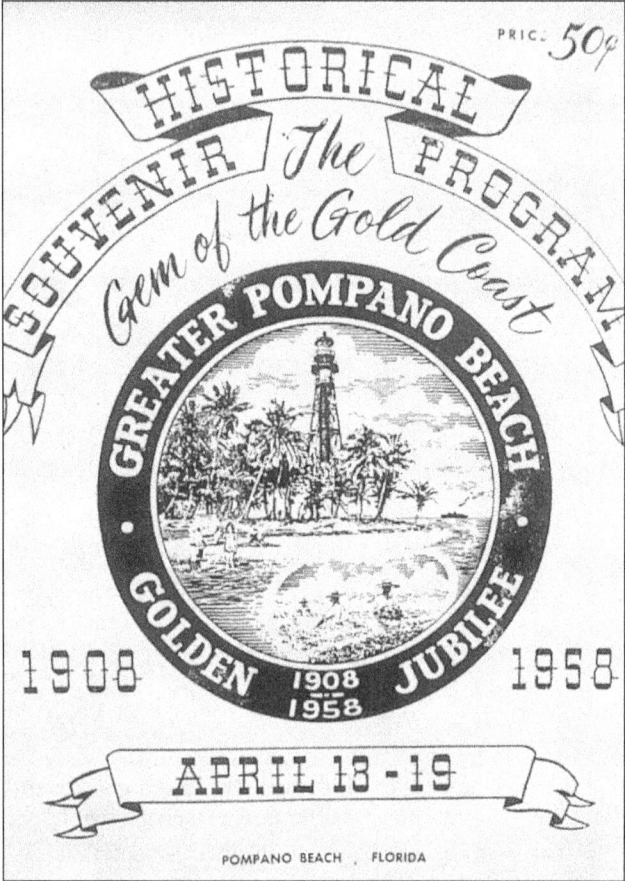

Pompano Beach celebrated its golden jubilee on April 18 and 19, 1958, with this Historical Souvenir Program. A chronicle of the City's past was included. Pompano was incorporated in 1908 and merged with Pompano Beach in 1947 to become the community it is today.

These anglers compete in the 1965 Pompano Beach Fishing Rodeo, an annual event held in May. It has become the largest sportfishing tournament in South Florida.

The second fire truck to serve Pompano Beach was built by American La France in 1948. Known as the "Invader," it was used until the 1970s. Still in mint condition, it stands in front of the Old Pompano Fire Station, now housing the Fire Museum, at Founders Park.

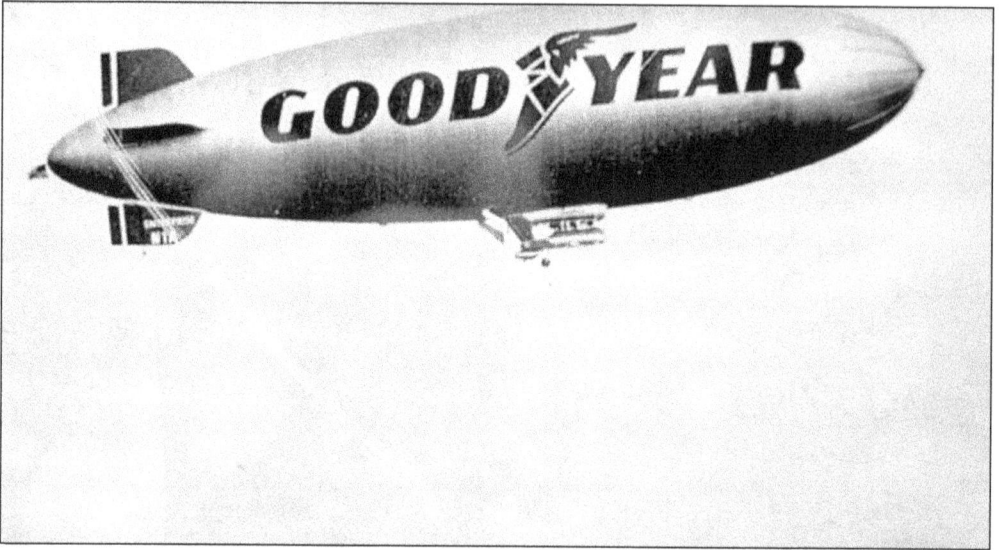

The Goodyear Airship *Enterprise* soars over Pompano Beach on November 8, 1979, as the City celebrated its arrival with a parade. It was christened by Mayor Emma Lou Olson. Below, an antique automobile and its occupants join the fun and thank Goodyear for choosing Pompano Air Park for its home. The Goodyear Blimp has provided considerable publicity and good will for the City.

Pompano Beach at one time served as a spring training home for the major leagues. The old Washington Senators and Texas Rangers used Municipal Stadium as their spring training home from 1961 to 1986. This major league game is being played March 1968, at Municipal Stadium.

Pompano Beach Municipal Stadium is shown here as it appears today. Although the park is still in use, it has seen better days. The City has not had a major league team for spring training since 1986.

North

Atlantic Blvd.

U. S. #1

Cypress Road

McNab Road

An aerial view of Pompano Beach in 1960 looks northward to the Atlantic Ocean. The Air Park is to the left in the background. Sprawl followed the beginning of housing development after Wold War II, although much vacant land remains. There were no high-rise buildings at the ocean during this period. The 1960 population of the community had increased to 15,992.

The proud members of the First AME Church, located at Northwest Third Avenue, pose for this rare group picture in the 1940s.

In 1977 the Pompano Beach City Commission consisted of the following members, from left to right: (Vice Mayor) J. Maxim Ryder, William J. Alsdorf, (Mayor) Betty Wistedt, Emma Lou Olson, and Herb Skolnick.

Men with heavy equipment work at the Fourteenth Street Bridge to connect the barrier island with the mainland in 1962. Since it was completed it has been one of the most heavily traveled bridges in South Florida . Note the heavy foliage surrounding the work area.

This tattered but proud American flag flies over Founders Park in Old Pompano. The flag flew on the SS *Pompano* submarine during World War II. The *Pompano* was launched in 1937 at Mare Island, California, was 300 feet long, and saw service in the Pacific Ocean.

Pictured looking west is the Fourteenth Street Bridge in 1968, crossing over the Intracoastal Waterway. State Road A1A is in the foreground east of the waterway. Considerable construction has since taken place along Fourteenth Street. The William J. Alsdorf Boat Launching Park is now located on the northwest side of the bridge.

The Pompano Beach Pier extends out to the Atlantic Ocean in this placid scene in 1969. It is a favorite place for tourists and residents to fish and enjoy dining in the Fisherman Wharf Restaurant to the left and the picnic area, not shown.

This is the first group of individuals initiated into the Elks Lodge 1898, Pompano Beach, April 17, 1953. The old "Casino" on Briny Avenue and Atlantic Boulevard was the initial home of the Elks. The second home of the Elks, from 1955 to 1984, was at 2300 Northeast Tenth Street, which was the original Three Sisters Motel and is presently the Super 8 Motel.

Groundbreaking ceremonies for the present site of the Pompano Beach Elks Lodge 1898 at 700 Northeast Tenth Street took place on August 15, 1982. The Elks leaders who presided were, from left to right, Don Downie, Don Burrie, Robert Grafton, Gil Van Horn, Dave Oscarson, and Martin Roberts.

Two boys interrupt their fishing to watch a boat travel up the Intracoastal Waterway as the Fourteenth Street Bridge is elevated. The time is 1968.

The vehicles at the intersection of Atlantic Boulevard (Route 814) and Federal HIghway reflect the modern development of Pompano Beach, February 7, 1969. Note the changes that have since taken place.

This December 7, 1969 scene looks south on North Federal Highway near Eighteenth Street and shows two lanes on each side. To the right of the highway the expanse of land that will be developed into the Pompano Fashion Square Mall can be seen. Note the Hudson gas station to the left advertising gasoline at $.31 9/10 per gallon.

These happy children are being entertained by a playful miniature horse under the watchful eyes of a volunteer supervisor at Pompano Park in 1968. The park opened in 1964 and has become the capital of harness racing in the United States. It remains fan friendly.

These patrons are broadening their intellectual horizons in the Pompano Beach Library at East Atlantic Boulevard and Northwest Thirteenth Avenue in 1970. It was opened in 1952 at a cost of $38,000 on land donated by William L. Kester. There are other branches at the beach and in the Northwest section of the city.

A large crowd was on hand for harness racing at the beginning of the 1968 Pompano Park winter season. The screened fence in front at the rail has been replaced by a brick wall. Also, there is now a glass enclosure in the center balcony just above the grandstand.

58

Looking north from Lake Santa Barbara, left, the Atlantic Boulevard Bridge can be seen in the distance as it crosses the Intracoastal Waterway. Lake Santa Barbara was once known as Hardy Lake because the Hardy family built the first house there. The Atlantic Ocean is at the northeast corner of the photo, and Harbor Village is at upper left.

Strolling on the beach is a favorite recreational activity for all. The expanse of sand and ocean comprise the city's most valuable asset. The bubbly-looking creatures in the foreground are called man-o-war and are blown onto shore by occasional wind and ocean currents. If touched their stingers can cause illness. This photo was taken in 1960.

These youngsters try their luck at the Fishing Pier hoping to catch "the big one" in 1968. Only two large condominiums can be seen in the background at this time. The population of Pompano Beach in 1970 had jumped to 39,012 and would continue to grow as development accelerated.

Four

POSTCARD IMAGES

This is a postcard view of the Pompano Beach Fishing Pier in the early 1970s when the building boom on the ocean was just beginning. The tall buildings on the left are the Sea Monarch and the Ocean Monarch. In the distance, center, is the Sands Harbor Hotel & Marina. To the right is the Granada House condominium.

Beautiful Storyland Park opened for children and the young-at-heart in November 1955, at 1101 South Federal Highway in Pompano Beach. The many attractions included Little Boy Blue, Jack and Jill, Peter Rabbit, Little Miss Muffett, and Humpty Dumpty. Storyland Park was eventually closed a decade later and razed.

The entrance to Storyland Park beckoned children to enjoy a fun day of make-believe. Storyland was located on Federal Highway, south of Atlantic Boulevard, across from Lake Santa Barbara.

The first colorful character a visitor met in Storyland Park was "Mary, Mary Quite Contrary" who explains here how her garden grows. Changing demographics in the 1960s caused the demise of this imaginative amusement park.

This postcard view of Storyland Park captures the colorful fantasy land of storybook people who fascinated young and old alike. The Storyland concept was created by Sydney Caswell and Al Hennessy.

The Pompano Beach Yacht Basin appears quaint and quiet in this 1950s photo. This facility has remained busy as it has catered to tourists and locals. The basin is located between the Intracoastal Waterway and Riverside Drive, north of Atlantic Boulevard. The Kester Brothers had helped develop the area into a tourist destination. In 1950 there were only 912 telephone connections, an indication of the relative lack of development.

The Oceanside Shopping Center, shown here, was a large part of the eastward commercial expansion to the ocean following World War II. The Yacht Basin can be seen in the background, center, at the Intracoastal Waterway. To the west is the city in the distance. Atlantic Boulevard meets State Road A1A (Ocean Boulevard) in the foreground to the right.

The famous Sea Watch Restaurant has won many awards for its fine food and service. This rustic landmark restaurant, featuring an interior nautical design in a tropical setting, is located on the ocean at the border of Pompano Beach and Fort Lauderdale. Since 1974 it has been noted for its native seafood.

As consumerism accelerated after World War II, "new" shopping malls, like the one shown here, were constructed to meet the increasing public demand for goods and services. This mall was considered so important that it was placed on a series of postcards.

Pompano Fashion Square is presented here on a postcard in a nighttime scene soon after it opened in January 1970. At the time it was one of largest shopping malls in the world.

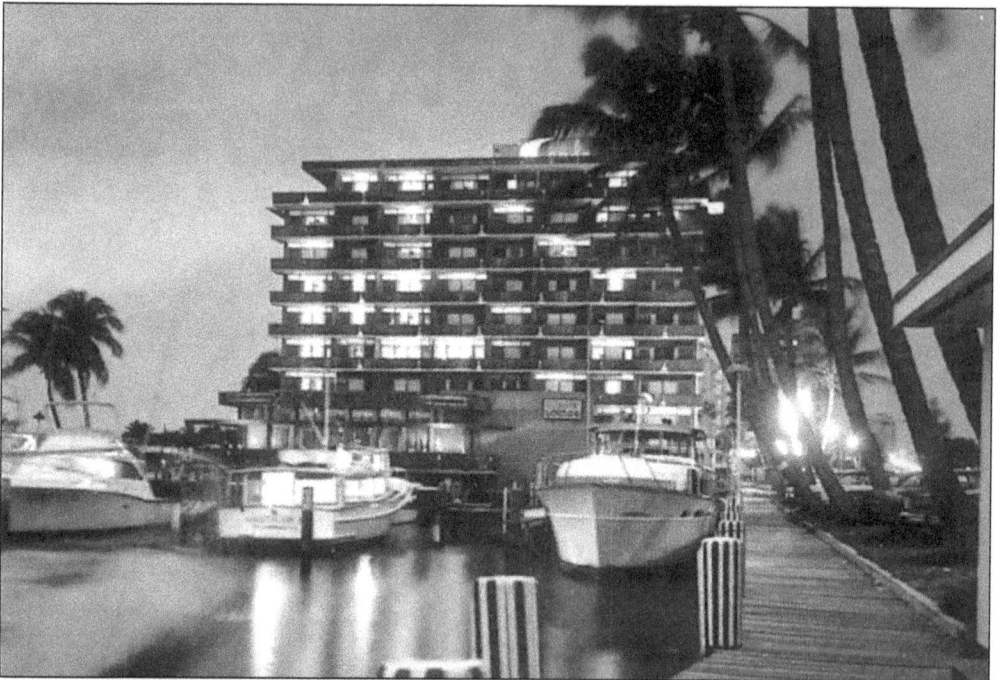

A fleet of fishing craft can be seen docked at the Pompano Beach Yacht Basin in this 1960s evening scene. Fishing has remained a great attraction for this South Florida city, which has often been called the "Gem of the Gold Coast." Fishes common to South Florida waters are tarpon, snook, snapper, sailfish, dolphin, and wahoo.

LAGO DEL MARE

Dr. Carlson's School of Corrective Motor Education, shown here, was based at Lago Del Mare in Pompano Beach during the winter season. There was also a summer session that was conducted at East Hampton, Long Island. In the lower panel, in the distance, the famous Hillsboro Lighthouse can be seen.

P.7—Hillsboro Light and Fishing Fleet Docks
Pompano Beach, Fla.

At the northern boundary of Pompano Beach lies the Hillsboro Inlet. This body of water leads from the Intracoastal Waterway to the Atlantic Ocean. The Hillsboro Lighthouse stands guard over the area in this 1960 scene. Opposite, at the dock in the foreground, charter boats wait to take tourists on fishing excursions.

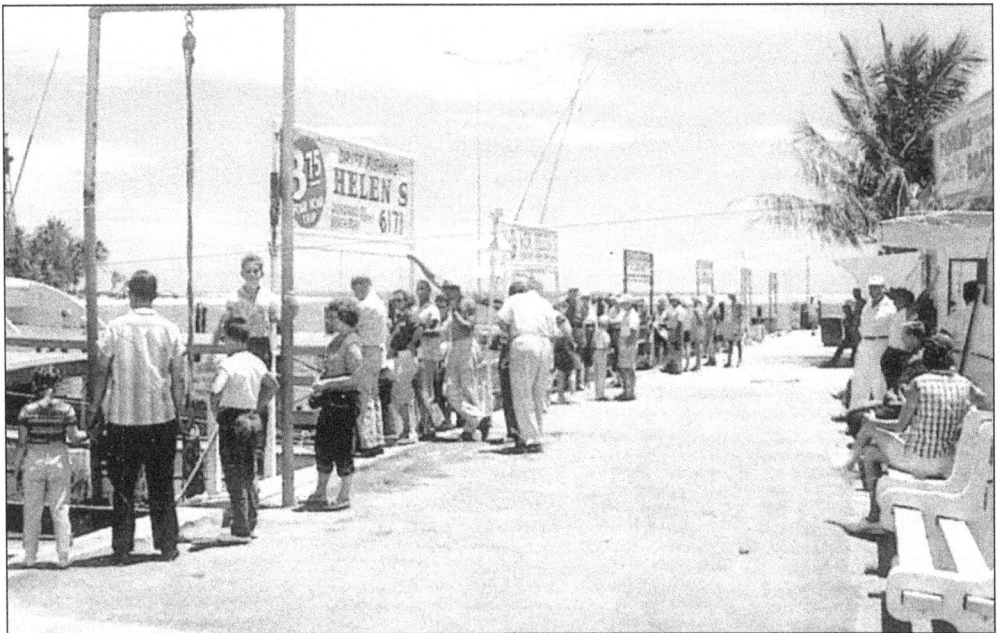

A crowd prepares to board the *Helen S* and other boats at the Hillsboro Inlet docks, Pompano Beach, to go deep-sea fishing in January 1963. At the extreme left is the Hillsboro Lighthouse. The crews of the excursion boats assisted newcomers and old salts with baiting hooks, marking catches, and handling prize catches.

This postcard captures a view of vacationers at the Chateau Pompano, a resort that was located on the Intracoastal Waterway at 1001 South Riverside Drive. It included all the vacation amenities, including boat docking facilities.

The Ocean Rest Motel Apartments provided oceanfront vacation living quarters. The resort, shown here in 1957 in a peaceful setting, was located at 21 South Ocean Boulevard, and it had a four-digit telephone number: Pompano 9190.

The Tropical Acres restaurant, shown here as it appeared in 1961, was one of the most famous landmark restaurants in Pompano Beach during this era. It was located at 2711 North Federal Highway but no longer exists at this site.

The staff of The French Place Restaurant at 360 East McNab Road posed proudly for this postcard image in the 1970s. The restaurant is family-owned and continues to be a popular eating place.

The old Ward's City Junior Department Store, as shown here in 1960, was a favorite shopping site during Pompano Beach's middle period. It was so popular, in fact, that it was placed on a postcard. But as shopping habits changed and the population shifted eastward, Ward's business contracted. Though the building still stands at Flagler and Northwest First Street, the store closed in 1999.

OCEAN HOLIDAY RESORT MOTEL

1350 No. Ocean Blvd.
Pompano Beach, Florida

The Ocean Holiday Resort Motel, pictured both above and below, at 1350 North Ocean Boulevard (State Road A1A) was just the type of vacation facility that William L. Kester envisioned when he promoted tourism in the 1930s for Pompano Beach. These 1964 scenes show vacationers relaxing and enjoying all the amenities at this beachfront motel.

The Sea Barge Restaurant, opposite the Pompano Public Golf Course, was famous for its broiled steaks and seafood. Patrons could dine in the popular Barge Room or the Salon, or they could dock and dine at the pier.

The Villa Nova Motel as it looked before South Ocean Boulevard (A1A) was widened and storm sewers and sidewalks were installed in the early 1990s. Such upgrading helped to modernize the area south of Atlantic Boulevard.

Two postcard views of the Surf Side Motel are presented here, one in the early 1960s (above) and the other in a contemporary view (below). Though located at 710 South Ocean Boulevard, it boasted of being 100 feet from the ocean; visitors actually had to cross Briny Avenue to get to the ocean. Note the differences that have taken place in the past 40 years.

The Pompano Beach Bank was established in 1934 and was located at 1101 East Atlantic Boulevard, as seen in this postcard. The bank is no longer in existence. A new Walgreen's store now occupies this site.

On the west side of South Ocean Boulevard (State Road A1A) at 1301 stands the Fairfield Santa Barbara Resort and Yacht Club. It is named for the lake to its rear where the first inhabitants settled. The Indian Mound Park is across the street.

Five

Historic Houses and More

The stately Harry McNab House at 1735 East Atlantic Boulevard awaits a refurbishing. It was built in 1926 and is important for local historical and architectural reasons. Its yellow brick exterior remains intact, and the house is classified as prairie vernacular architecture. Also unique to Pompano Beach is the Robert McNab House, not shown, opposite this home at 1736 East Atlantic Boulevard.

This bungalow-style house was built for pioneer businessman Frank Austin by Gus Hardin in 1924 at 410 Northeast Fifth Avenue. It boasts original oak floors, cabinets, and chandeliers. Its classical straight lines adds to its appealing appearance.

The Wallace Robinson House at 400 Northeast Fifth Avenue was built in 1924 and represents Moorish Revival architecture, which had a brief lifespan in South Florida. Unique to Pompano Beach, it is characterized by parapets, a flat roof, and semicircular windows.

This giant five-stop German Votteler organ with pipes, at right, was added to the music room of the Horace Robinson House at 405 Northeast Fifth Avenue in 1932. Wednesday morning musicales were held in this comfortable setting, paving the way for the growth of the Broward Opera Guild and Symphony Orchestra.

The Horace Robinson House at 405 Northeast Fifth Avenue was built of Dade County pine in 1924. The backyard contains the city's first above-ground poured concrete swimming pool. It is the home of Broward County's first symphony orchestra and opera.

The Harley "Cap" Campbell House, shown here, was built in 1910 at Northeast First Street and rolled on logs in the 1920s to its present location at 300 Northeast Fourth Street. Although modifications were made by later owners, the Campbell House retains its architectural integrity and the warmth of Southern hospitality. Campbell was a pioneer farmer, politician, and realtor.

Built in 1939 during the Great Depression, the Bo Giddens House was unique in being the first house built in Pompano to receive an FHA loan. The original cost of construction was $3,000, with an additional cost of $500 for land. Giddens was a prominent businessman and politician. The house is located at Northeast Third Street and Northeast Third Avenue.

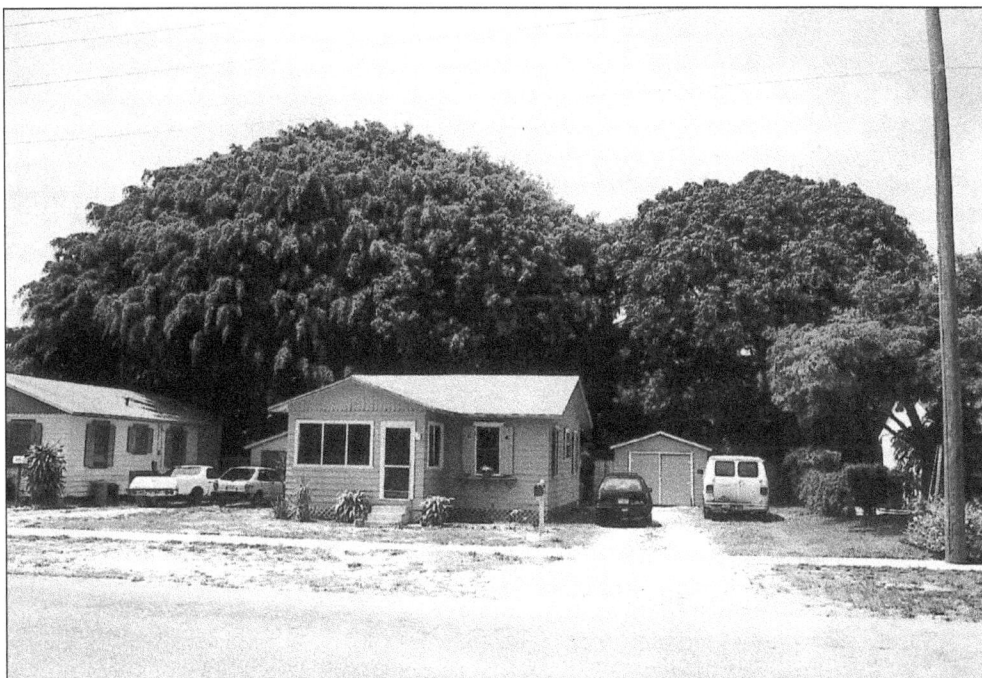

This neat Kester Cottage, center, is located at 609 Northeast First Street. Formerly a vacation cottage at the beach, it was moved to its present location to serve as a permanent residence. There are a few remaining Kester Cottages scattered around the city, and they serve as reminders of the early Pompano Beach tourist industry.

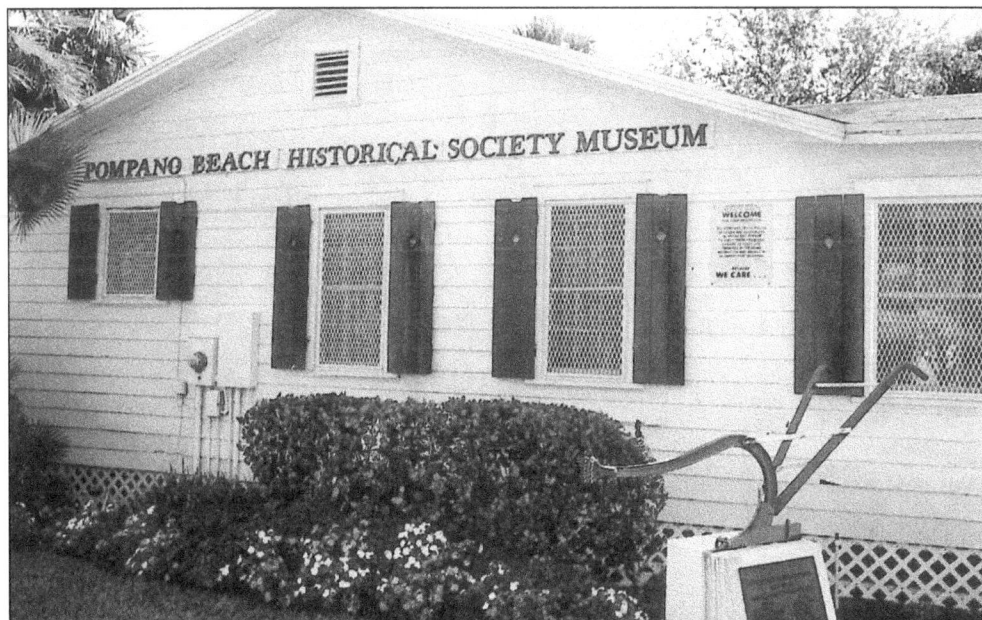

A Kester Cottage at Founders Park, shown here, houses the Pompano Beach Historical Museum. The cottage was moved from the beach area and restored in period furniture. It served as a vacation cottage during the 1930s and 1940s. Note the plow in front; it symbolizes the agricultural beginnings of Pompano.

The City Utilities Department celebrated its 75th anniversary of providing water to residents. Well House Number One, or Pump House, located here at Northeast Second Street and Northeast Third Avenue, was built in 1926 to protect the pump and motor equipment for Well Number One. The structure remains standing today at Founders Park for historic preservation.

There are two bocci courts at Founders Park. These "snowbirds" from the North engage in weekly competitions during the winter season. To the left is the Dick and Miriam Hood Center.

These Kester Cottages were located along the ocean, north of Atlantic Boulevard. By the 1940–1941 season the Kester Ocean Homes, as they were then called, had a separate dining room in all the two-story cottages. Of the more than 100 that were built, about 10 remain scattered around the city. Two are at Founders Park.

The Bevill building in Old Pompano at Flagler Avenue was built in 1934 and is an example of Mission-style architecture. Inspired by the Spanish Mission–style churches, it was popular during the 1920s and was noted for its simplicity. At one time Bo and Mattie Giddens owned and operated a restaurant here.

The Blanche Ely Educational Museum honors the prominent high school principal and civic leader who greatly influenced the development of Pompano Beach. The museum is set in the Ely three-bedroom home located at Northwest Fifteenth Street and Northwest Sixth Avenue.

The Mt. Calvary Baptist Church at 800 Northwest Eighth Avenue is the oldest church in Pompano Beach and Broward County, having been founded the fourth Sunday in May 1902, six years before the City was incorporated. Esther Rolle spoke to hundreds of people here during a ceremony on March 16, 1981, after a triumphant parade along the avenue that was named for her.

This panoramic view of the sanctuary is the focal point of the St. Martin-in-the Fields Episcopal Church located south of the Atlantic Boulevard Bridge and east of the Intracoastal Waterway. The church was built in 1962. Pompano Beach's population had risen to 15,992 by 1960.

This postcard image shows the Wallace A. Robinson House in Old Pompano during the 1930s. Robinson was the manager of the Hammon Development Company, which laid a rock road and drained the land around Coral Springs, Margate, and Coconut Creek. The area became one of the largest bean farms in South Florida.

The First Baptist Church of Pompano Beach was opened May 4, 1915, when 21 people gathered to worship at 138 Northeast First Street. The Reverend S.P. Mahoney was the Church's founding pastor. Some of the original congregation members were Rachel Hardin, Kitty Hardy, Mr. and Mrs. Edward Cook, and Mrs. A. J. McGaughy. Today there are over 1,500 active members.

The First United Methodist Church at 210 Northeast Third Street was completed in 1939 and traces its roots back to 1908. As an example of Gothic architecture, it has retained its design integrity even though an addition on its north side was not compatible with its original style.

The John Knox Village, at the center and top of this photo, comprises 62 acres of land and is a nationally accredited lifetime and continuing-care retirement community of 1,000 residents. Home styles include garden and lakeside villas, and apartments in the low, mid, and high-rise categories. It has attracted active seniors for more than three decades.

The Rolle House at 721 Northwest Third Avenue (Esther Rolle Avenue) is where actress Esther Rolle grew up as part of an Old Pompano family. The house is a good example of Bahamian-style, wood-frame vernacular architecture. A historic survey revealed more structures were identified with this design than any other. These houses are rectilinear in form and noted for their simplicity.

Mildred Swain and her family lived in this house in the Northwest section of Old Pompano. As a wood-frame vernacular structure, it does not adhere to any academic style and was the typical method of construction used by the early pioneers. Local materials were used to adapt to local conditions, and the structure was built on a masonry or stone foundation.

During the Great Depression the Christian Pallbearers Society was formed to defray the expense of funeral bills for its members. Its building is shown here. The society was similar to an immigrant mutual aid society as a type of insurance to cover emergency sickness and funeral expenses. Society premiums ranged from a quarter to a dollar a week.

The Pompano Park grandstand and race course are shown here during the construction phase in 1963. The standard bred harness track opened February 4, 1964. This development contributed to an increase of tourism and population growth in Pompano Beach, which reached 37,724 six years later.

The Sample-McDougald House is shown at 3161 North Dixie Highway, before it was moved to its new site at 450 Northeast Tenth Street, Pompano Beach. This two-story classical revival house has 17 rooms and 11-foot ceilings. It is listed on the National Register of Historic Places.

An artist's rendering of the restored Sample-McDougald House is presented here. The house was built in 1916 by Albert Neal Sample, a farmer and a Broward County commissioner. In 1943 William D. and Sarah McDougald purchased the house and directed their farming operations from it. The McDougalds donated the house to the Sample-McDougald House Preservation Society, Inc., which will operate it as a living museum.

Actress Esther Rolle is buried at this grave site in Westview Cemetery located at Northwest Fifteenth Avenue between Powerline Road and Copans Road. Rolle was raised in Pompano and was proud of her hometown where many of her relatives still reside. Among her many stage, screen, and television roles, she is most famous for role as Florida Evans in the award-winning television comedy *Good Times*.

The old commercial section of Pompano is a one-part block on North Flagler Avenue, between Northeast First Street and Northeast Third Street, facing the Florida East Coast Railroad. The stores were united in function and served the business needs of the community. A once-thriving Ward's City, shown here on North Flagler, closed its doors in the late 1990s as demographics and shopping patterns changed.

The changing skyline of Pompano Beach dominates this scene as condominiums rise above State Road A1A, south of Atlantic Boulevard, looking towards the Atlantic Ocean. At the extreme right, partially hidden, is the Renaissance II, to its left is the Renaissance I, and above it in the center is the Claridge. The Fishing Pier is barely visible in the distance at upper left. In the foreground is The Seasons, a retirement residence by Hyatt.

Six

POMPANO HAPPENINGS

Pompano Beach proudly participated in the nation's bicentennial celebration. Here Congressman Paul Rogers, left, presents the American Revolution Bicentennial Flag at City Hall, October 17, 1975, to Mayor William S. Alsdorf, right.

This announcement with logo on the lower left shows the First Annual Fishing Rodeo in Pompano Beach, May 6–8, 1966. Anglers hold their prize-wining trophies in this first competition. Over the years the Fishing Rodeo has helped the ecology as it joined in sinking over 25 ships and other approved materials off the coast of Pompano Beach as artificial reefs to increase habitats for marine life. The fishing rodeo has become South Florida's largest and richest sportfishing tournament.

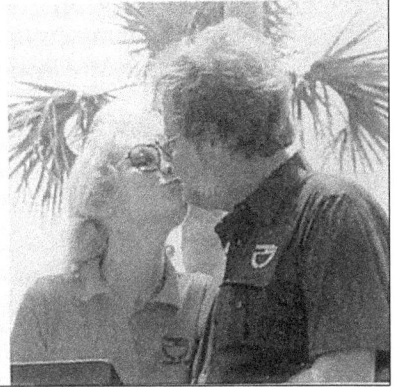

Participants, above, in the original Fishing Rodeo enjoy the event's camaraderie. Today nearly 1,000 anglers aboard more than 250 boats compete in this local family event. All profits are returned to the marine environment. The Fishing Rodeo has contributed to the funding of the marine research program at Ely High School called Project Ocean Exploration, which gives students the opportunity to investigate Broward County's coastal habitats.

These happy people participate in the groundbreaking ceremony for the construction of Pompano Park Raceway on June 19, 1963. Frederick Van Lennep, the fourth person standing from the right in the front row, and wife, Frances, standing at his left, introduced harness racing to South Florida. The Van Lenneps were owners of Castleton Farms in Lexington, Kentucky, and Wolverine Raceway in Detroit, Michigan.

Pompano Beach City Commissioners, from left to right, William J. Alsdorf, Robert Fuller, Mayor Edward J. Stack, George Fiver, and Bill Pelski join in the ribbon-cutting ceremony for the dedication of the new Fourteenth Street Bridge on January 31, 1968.

96

Sixty acres of the Pompano Beach Airport property were purchased by Leonard Farber in 1966 for the construction of Pompano Fashion Square, as conceived above in this layout design. Federal Highway (US 1) is to the right. On the northern boundary of the shopping center is Copans Road. At the time it was a state-of-the-art shopping mall and one of the largest in the world.

Shovels are flying for the groundbreaking event for Pompano Fashion Square on August 1, 1968. Standing with shovels, from left to right, are Vice Mayor Bob Fuller, Commissioner George Fivek, General Manager Leonard Farber, Mayor Edward J. Stack, Commissioner William J. Alsdorf, and City Manager Ellsworth Hoppe.

A large group of dignitaries and other interested persons turned out for the groundbreaking ceremony for Pompano Fashion Square, August 1, 1968. Chairing this special event was Bud Boyer, left, facing the guests.

RESIDENTS AND GUESTS
COULD HAVE DANCED ALL NIGHT

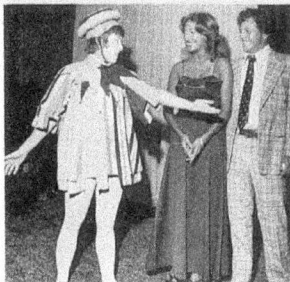

Guests receive courtly greeting.

Mr. and Mrs. Jess Dorkin.

Tommy Mercer and his orchestra.

Mr. and Mrs. Ernest Nelson, left, and Mr. and Mrs. Russ Colley.

Mr. and Mrs. James F. Douglas, left, with Mr. and Mrs. Jack Tropp.

Mr. and Mrs. Harvey E. Ramsey and party.

Ralph DeRoy, left, with Rita Kelner, Mrs. DeRoy, Mr. and Mrs. George Marks.

A queenly hostess and court jester.

Mrs. Robert Jones, Mrs. Young, the Herman Wasserbergers and guests.

Some of the 400 residents and guests in the Versailles Room of the Renaissance I condominium are enjoying the inaugural Gala Ball, February 2, 1975. They dined and danced to the music of Tommy Mercer, upper right corner. The construction of the Renaissance I at 1360 South Ocean Boulevard was part of the building boom that occurred on the beach in this period of the 1970s.

The luxurious 28-story Renaissance I condominium, front, and the Renaissance II, partially hidden to its left, were built in 1974 and 1976, respectively. Such high-rise construction on the ocean helped to reshape Pompano Beach.

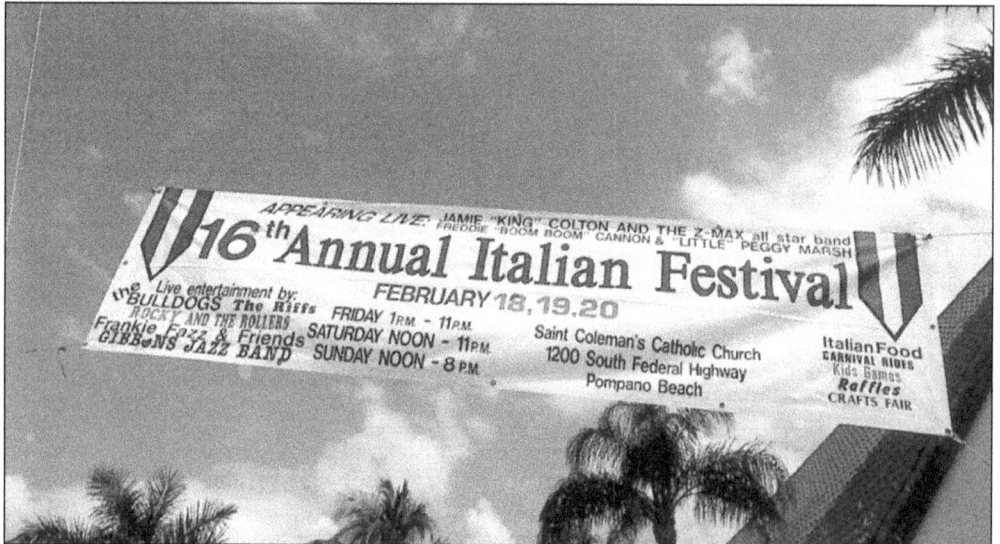

One of the most successful local ongoing family events is the Annual Italian Festival conducted by volunteers of St. Coleman's Catholic Church. This banner on the church grounds at South Federal Highway announces the event for the year 2000. Note the list of entertainers on the banner.

The annual Holiday Boat Parade is held each December in Pompano Beach and attracts hundreds of participants and thousands of spectators. At the top is the famous boat, the *Helen S-VI*. The parade began in 1962. Condominiums and homes along the Intracoastal Waterway, as seen in the bottom photo, add to the festive spirit with brightly lit decorations for the season. The event is also presented on television.

This vividly decorated boat with toy and live soldiers makes its way along the Intracoastal Waterway during the 1994 Holiday Boat Parade. The event has become a tradition that boasts a proud community spirit. By 1980 Pompano Beach population had risen to 52,618 and to 72,411 by 1990.

Mr. and Mrs. Santa Claus wave from the bow of their boat during the 1992 Pompano Beach Holiday Boat Parade. Fort Lauderdale has a similar event that is also presented annually in December.

Pompano Beach's very own Esther Rolle receives an Emmy for her leading role as Florida Evans in the television series *Good Times*. An outstanding citizen in her right and proud of her hometown roots, she starred as the mother of a household that espoused traditional middle class values and a strong sense of family.

The Reverend Martin Cassidy, pastor of the Assumption Catholic Church, turns over the first shovel of dirt for the construction of the Parish's new church on December 20, 1992. From left to right in the front are Reverend Michael Krulak, an altar boy, Auxiliary Bishop Augustin A. Roman of the Miami Diocese, and Reverend Cassidy.

The new Assumption Catholic Church, located at 2001 South Ocean Boulevard, takes shape during the construction phase. The old mission parish church/auditorium at rear was built in 1952 at a cost of $68,000. It was razed in 1994.

The dedication of the Assumption Church took place on Saturday, April 23, 1994, and was attended by parishioners and guests. Rev. Edward A. McCarthy, archbishop of Miami, presided. Most Reverend Joseph Cassidy, archbishop of Tuam, Ireland, was the homilist.

The Assumption Church arrives at completion. The Mission Church was served by Fr. John Cotter (1950–1951) and Fr. M.J. Fogarty (1951–1959). The following priests have served as pastor: Fr. Patrick D. O'Brien (1959–1964); Msgr. Thomas O'Donovan (1964–1968); Msgr. Robert W. Shiefen (1968–1970); Msgr. Rowan T. Rastatter (1970–1991); and Fr. Martin Cassidy (1991–)

Popular harness driver Wally Hennessey celebrates his 5,000th win at the winners' circle as track announcer Larry Albano (right), publicity director Carol Scott (left), and brother Danny Hennessey look on. The event took place at Pompano Park on June 29, 2000.

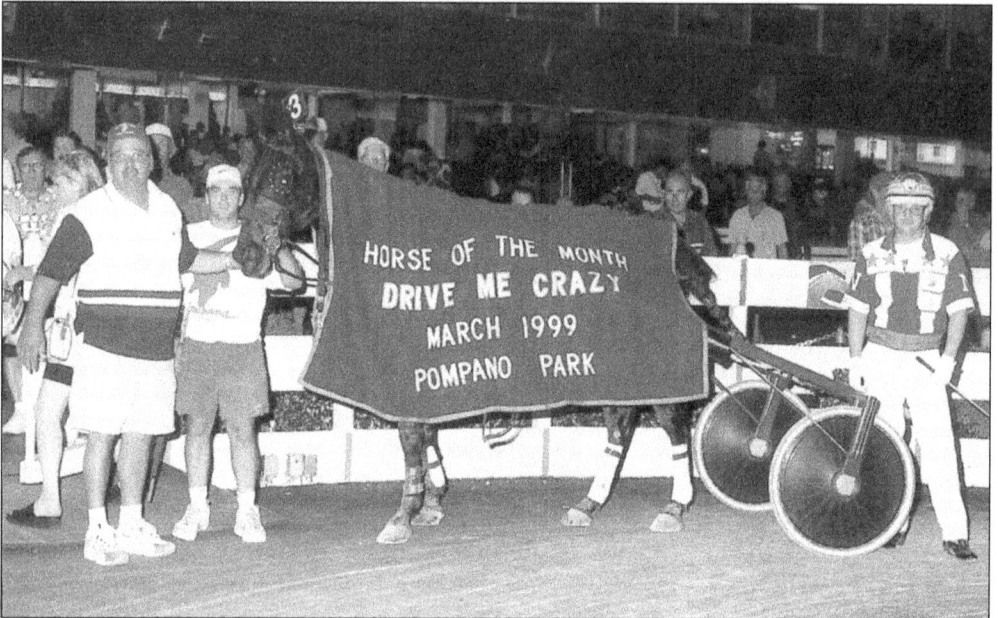

Harness driver George Napolitano Jr., right, and Joe Napolitano, far left, stand with Pompano Park horse of the month "Drive Me Crazy" for March 1999.

The Annual Seafood Festival attracts more than 50,000 people to the beach at East Atlantic Boulevard each April. Pompano Beach has long been famous for its fishing and seafood delights. These people enjoy a concert during a recent Seafood Festival.

The Seafood Festival has become a popular gathering on the beach where fun, food, and entertainment are enjoyed by thousands of visitors and residents. The Pompano Beach Fishing Pier is in the background and the Hillsboro Lighthouse can be seen in the distance.

107

A proud David Jackson, left, celebrated his 100th birthday with his family on March 13, 1983. At that time he had 10 children, 69 grandchildren, 92 great grandchildren, and 6 great-great grandchildren. Jackson worked on the first railroad that was built in Pompano.

Seven

POMPANO BEACH TODAY

There can be no doubt of the significance that water sports plays in the lifestyle and economy of Pompano Beach. This scene of the Hidden Harbour Marina at Northeast Twenty-third Street demonstrates the popularity of boating.

Organized in 1947, the present Pompano Beach Chamber of Commerce building was dedicated in that year at 2200 East Atlantic Boulevard on land donated by Mrs. W.H. McNab. The chamber has contributed to the growth in tourism, industry, business, and community spirit.

This sign identifies McNab Park, located behind the chamber of commerce building. The park was donated by W.H. McNab and R.A. McNab following World War II.

Shuffleboard is a popular activity at McNab Park. These players compete on a regular basis and are shown here concentrating on their game.

These smiling children enjoy a day in the park at summer camp. There are 11 active parks and 5 passive parks in Pompano Beach among the many other recreational facilities programs available all year round.

The Oceanside Shopping Center at the intersection of Atlantic Boulevard and State Road A1A was constructed during the period of eastward growth and development in the 1960s. In recent years business activity has declined here and the area has been rezoned for high-rise development.

This sign marks the location of Kester Park at Northeast Ninth Avenue and Sixth Street, named for William L. Kester who settled in Pompano in 1923 and who became an early City booster. The park contains 8.4 acres featuring baseball, football, and soccer fields, as well as a playground, a sand volleyball court, and a picnic area.

Tourism is an important industry in Pompano Beach. These vehicles are used to sweep and collect debris on the beach on a daily basis in order to maintain a clean environment, as well as to prevent sand erosion. A condominium dominates the background.

Admiralty Towers condominium stands facing the beach at 750 North Ocean Boulevard. Behind and to the lower left is St. Gabriel Catholic Church. This aerial view faces west from the ocean.

Looking north from Sea Ranch Lakes, lower left, in this contemporary scene, Pompano Beach can be seen extending along the waterfront. The Intracoastal Waterway is in the background to the left. The fishing pier is barely visible in the upper right corner.

A happy group of John Knox Village retirees/residents enjoys a meal in the patio dining room, also a popular place for socializing. They are a part of 1,000 senior citizens living there.

This modern marina at Pompano Beach is located north of Atlantic Boulevard and east of the bridge at the Intracoastal Waterway. The Atlantic Ocean can be seen in the background to the right between two condominiums.

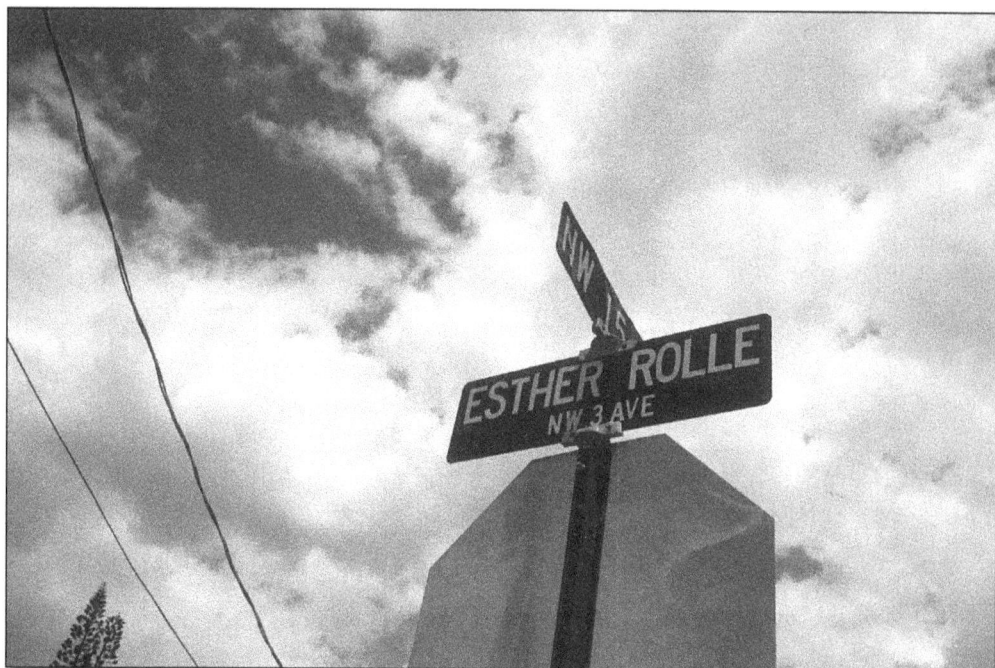

This street sign in northwest Pompano pays tribute to famous actress Esther Rolle, the star of the television series *Good Times*. Esther was the daughter of a Pompano pioneer family who worked at farming. Her brother, Cornelius, served the City for many years and his daughter, Janice Rolle, has been a leading librarian.

The bust of Blanche General Ely is part of the Ely Educational Museum. It was sculpted by George E. Gadson in honor of the outstanding educational leader. She was born in January 7, 1904, in Reddick, Florida, and died December 18, 1993, in Pompano Beach.

The above photo announces the Blanche Ely High School, while the photo below designates Blanche Ely Avenue (Northwest Sixth Avenue) in honor of the accomplished educator. She and her husband, Professor Joseph A. Ely, became a dynamic educational leadership team. She came to Pompano Beach when she was a young adult and was appointed principal to a two-room schoolhouse on Hammond Road that later became Coleman Elementary School. The high school in Northwest Pompano was named for her.

Pompano Beach is a diverse community known for its many ethnic groups. The Islamic Center of South Florida, shown here, has been at 507 Northeast Sixth Street for nearly two decades. It contains a mosque, school, library, and meeting hall for its growing population. In the lower photo students display the trophies they earned for outstanding achievement in the Islamic faith.

Carol Scott holds the "Number 1" cloth of Niatross, one of the most popular standard-bred horses ever to race and was also a member of Harness Racing Hall of Fame. Walnridge Farm manager Chris Coyne, left, holds Niatross while announcer Gary Seibel looks on during this ceremony at Pompano Park on December 6, 1997.

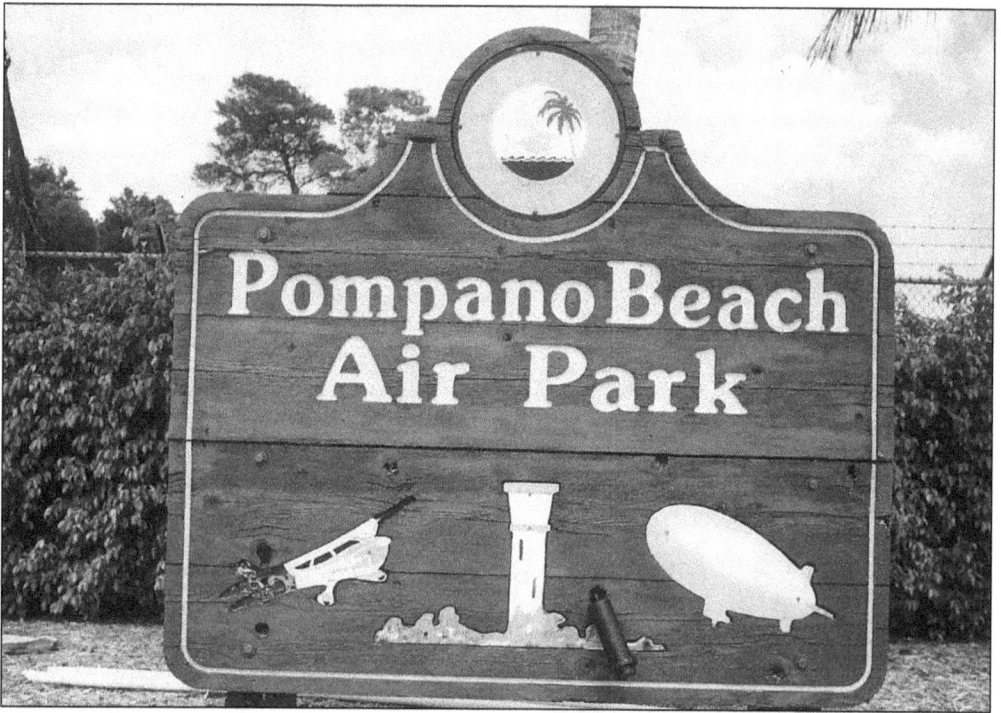

The Pompano Beach Air Park is owned and operated by the City for the general aviation needs of Broward County. This valuable facility, identified by this sign, is located in the heart of South Florida's Gold Coast and is within easy access of recreational and business activities.

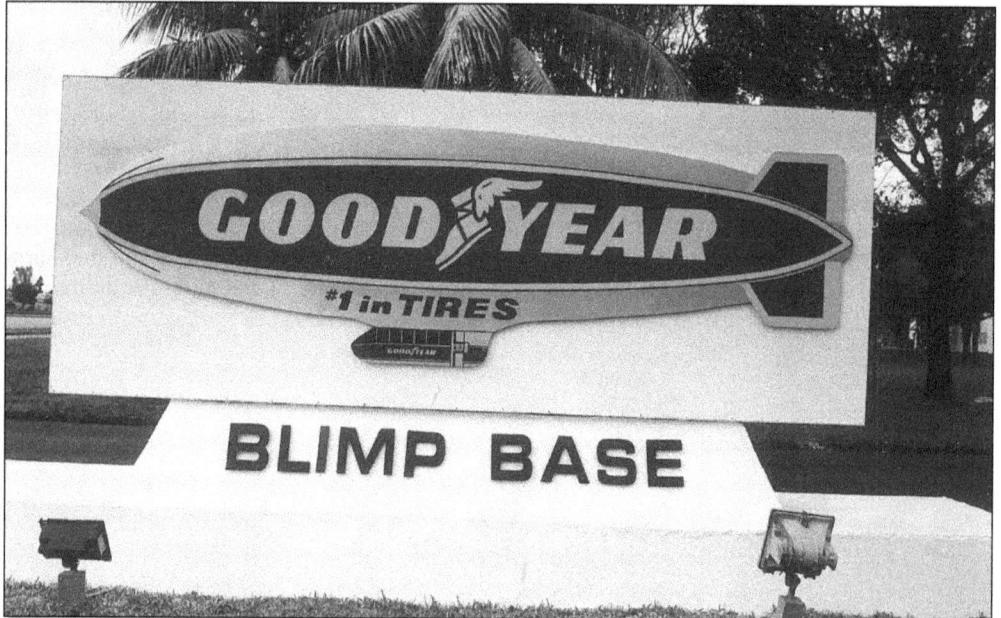

The Goodyear Blimp has been stationed at Pompano Beach since 1979. This sign can be seen at the west side of Pompano Air Park. The Blimp hangar measures 45,000 square feet. The Blimp provides aerial television coverage of sporting events. It also flashes public service messages with its 3,780 light boards attached to each of its sides.

For more than 75 years Goodyear Blimps have adorned the skies. This Goodyear Blimp, "Stars and Stripes," was constructed in Pompano Beach and has brought much pride and notoriety to the city. At 192 feet long, it was christened at Pompano Air Park on March 8, 2001. The air ship is a familiar sight as it floats over Pompano Beach and at major sporting events.

These two contemporary scenes highlight the public attractions at the beach. Above are Fisherman's Wharf, featuring an oceanfront restaurant and lounge, and the fishing pier, which is the longest pier in Florida and extends 1,080 feet into the ocean. Below are recreational facilities for children and other amenities for the family, such as a picnic area.

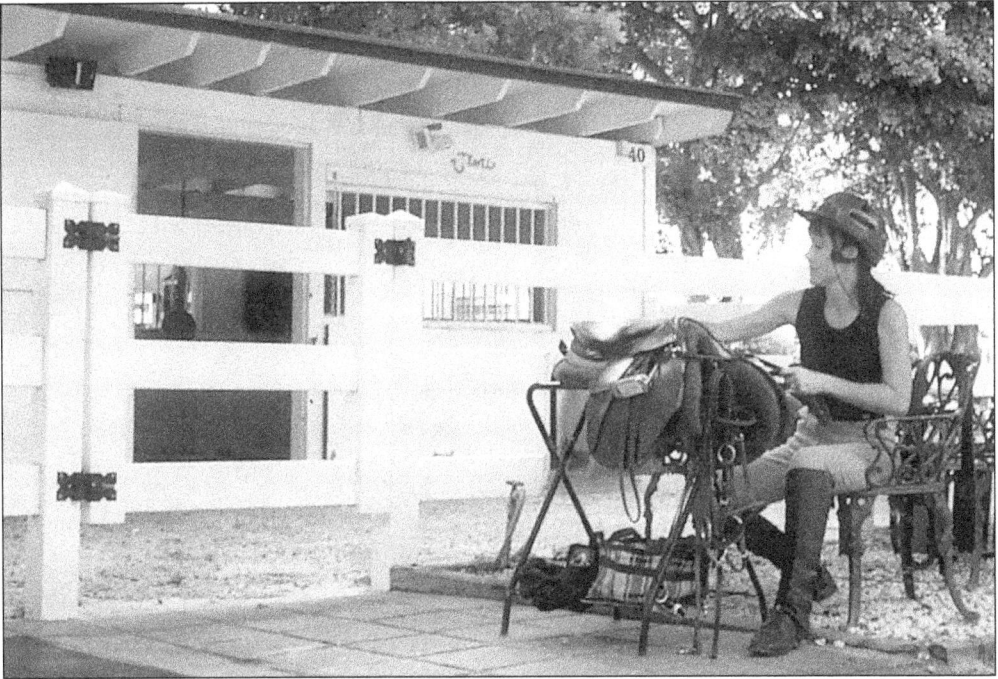

Pompano's ten-acre Sand and Spurs Equestrian Park is located at Northeast Fifth Street near the Goodyear Blimp Base. It has been there since the early 1950s. The park offers an exercise and riding ring, open field, picnic area, grills, and restrooms. In this photo Pam Livecchi cleans her saddle after a ride at the park.

Looking west from Southeast Thirteenth Street and Hibiscus Avenue, Lake Santa Barbara can be seen from the site of the historic Indian Mound. This quiet setting is just west of busy South Ocean Boulevard (AIA).

"This is an opportunity to reflect on a man who made a big dent in the fabric of America. This ceremony is just a small sacrifice for us to pay tribute to the contributions of Martin Luther King."

- Former Commissioner Pat Larkins

Honoring the work of civil rights leader Dr. Martin Luther King Jr. has become a local tradition. Here Pat Larkins, right, who spent 20 years on the Pompano Beach City Commission, addresses an audience during an inspirational program at Blanche Ely High School. Young people display their respect. Street signs of Dr. King's and Esther Rolle's names are appropriately included in this scene.

Florida's lieutenant governor Frank Brogan, center, visited Pompano Beach to coordinate partnership programs between the state and local government. From left to right are Vice Mayor Herb Skolnick, Commissioner Kay McGinn, Brogran, Commissioner Bob Shelley, and Mayor William Griffin. Not shown is Commissioner Ed Phillips.

The Old Pompano neighborhood has had a colorful past, and it has sought to preserve that past. The City created the Historic Preservation Board to designate historical sites. As a result, the Old Pompano Civic Association organized a Historic Homes Tour for March 24, 2001. This group of visitors waits to enter the Cap Campbell House at 300 Northeast Fourth Street during the tour.

In Memory
of
Off. Scott A. Winters
March 30, 1962 - July 29, 1990

First Police Officer
Killed in The Line of Duty

Pompano Beach Police Department

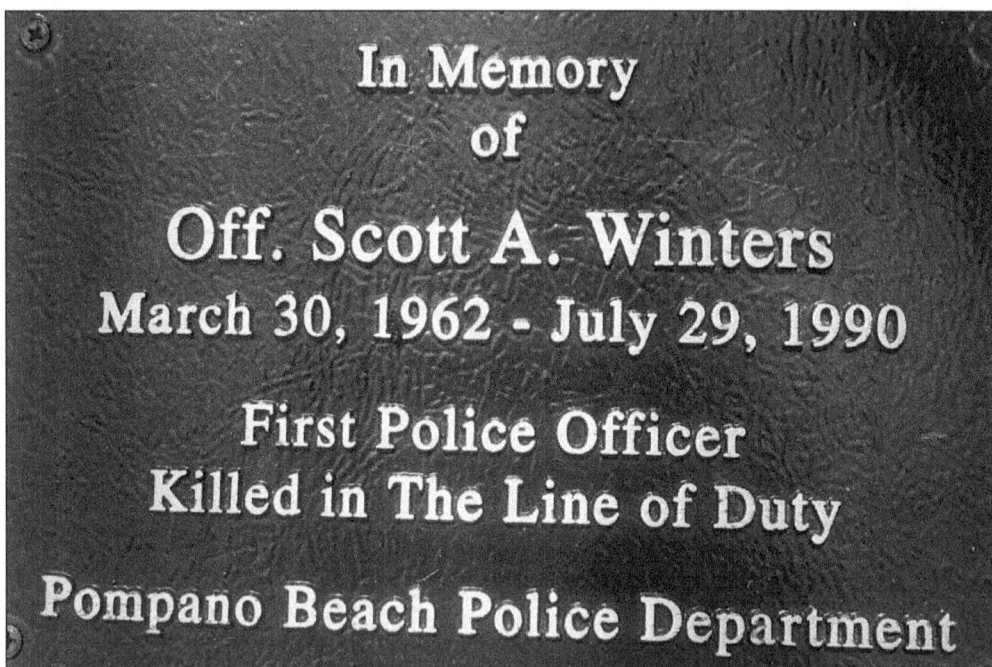

Scott A. Winters is the only Pompano Beach police officer killed in the line of duty. The City's leaders expressed their deep appreciation by renaming Sunset Park, located at 1200 North Riverside Drive, the Scott A. Winters Memorial Park. This bronze plaque, above, has been placed in the park as a permanent reminder of his sacrifice. The scenic view, below, looks west with the Intracoastal Waterway just beyond the park, south of the Fourteenth Street Bridge.

These members of San Isidro Catholic Church at 2310 Martin Luther King Boulevard gather for a group photo during a religious retreat in July 1999. Iglesia Catolica, a multicultural parish, has celebrated mass in English and Spanish since 1970. A new sanctuary was completed and dedicated in August 1999.

This composition of images was created and presented by the Greater Pompano Beach Chamber of Commerce. It represents the variety of attractions that have drawn residents and tourists to the area of South Florida. Pompano Beach has had several designations, including "Gem of the Gold Coast," "Heart of the Gold Coast," the "New Playground of America," and "Pleasure Boating Paradise."

Visit us at
arcadiapublishing.com
···